THE

FINAL

CALL

McDougal & Associates
*Servants of Christ and Stewards of the
Mysteries of God*

THE

FINAL

CALL

ARE WE PRESENTLY RECEIVING THE FINAL CALL OF THE SPIRIT?

BY
JERRY FITCH

Published by:

McDougal & Associates
18896 Greenwell Springs Road
Greenwell Springs, LA 70739

www.ThePublishedWord.com

McDougal & Associates is an organization dedicated to
spreading the Gospel of the Lord Jesus Christ to as many
people as possible in the shortest time possible.

ISBN: 978-1-950398-04-1

Printed in the U.S., the U.K. and Australia
For Worldwide Distribution

DEDICATION

In these days we are living in, I sense an urgency in the hearts and lives of those around me who are expecting something great to occur. We often define our expectations by our upraising in church culture, often by our present circumstances and often by our personal desires. It seems to me that maybe all of these will ultimately hold truth. Whatever the case, something good is about to happen.

It is for that cause that I dedicate this writing to my lovely wife and confidant—Monique. She stands as a strong bulwark in my life to ensure my continual pursuit in Christ and His Kingdom. Her trust is overwhelming, her guidance is immeasurable, her words are sure. A lifetime with her will prove that success will be attained and happiness fulfilled.

I thank you, my Love, for who you are and whose you are in my life. Together, not only can we; together we will!

Then, Now & Always!

Jerry

CONTENTS

Foreword by Marvin Gorman

The message of this book challenges every Christian to take an honest look at where we are as a Church in this present hour. It is a straight-forward message, pointing out clearly the ills confronting us all. However, it does not leave us helpless and hopeless with the problems, but points us to the move of God that brings hope.

It is a must that we listen to the cry of God's Spirit concerning His work in this last-day harvest. This book contains a powerful teaching that I pray will awaken many to action.

Reverend Marvin E. Gorman
New Orleans, Louisiana

INTRODUCTION

Each culture has indigenous characteristics that distinguish it from any other culture. Its identification to a particular ethnic group is clearly defined and understood as pertaining solely to that group. So it is with the readers of this book. You are part of a unique generation of people.

Why do I say that? Because we have turned a critical corner and are now living in a whole new time. This is a whole new century. In fact, it is a whole new millennium. Because of this, we are now fulfilling prophetic utterances of the Word of God that have been designed distinctly for this particular time and for this particular generation. Prophecy is so clear that it would be nearly impossible to mistake what is being declared.

And yet, this generation, as is with all generations, must find its purpose in Christ. Much of the cry of the Church today is for unity. Meetings are held to discuss how to obtain unity. Special luncheons are called, ministries who specialize in a message concerning unity are invited to come and "lead" us into achieving unity. Even with all the efforts to unity, however, this generation stands out as the most divided and confused generation of all times. I submit to you that it is not unity that we need, it is purpose. Let's find God's purpose in our lives and unity will follow. You see, purpose brings unity. Unity is simply a by-product of purpose. Therefore, as we are able, as a church, to define our purpose and gravitate toward that purpose, unity will follow.

> **Let's find God's purpose
> in our lives, and
> unity will follow!**

Introduction

God has given us an area of influence that we must discover and begin to function in order to fulfill His eternal purpose. May I say to you that just as there are evil spirits assigned to territories, the various elements of the Body of Christ have been assigned to specific territories to fulfill God's purpose. We have been given "territories of purpose" by God, and we must know our purpose in Him to fulfill His plan.

This is not an unreachable or unattainable goal. I now speak to you prophetically: in the foreseeable future, the church will begin to reach toward her purpose and make inroads into the plan of God in the earth for His glory.

God is speaking to the potential of His people today in this day of visitation. As God's people prophesy or speak in agreement with the Word that He is speaking in a given area, He makes an adjustment in the atmosphere at the declaration of His Word, the enemy becomes subject to that Word, and things begin to happen! In this way, God sets the stage for His Word to come to pass!

> **God is speaking to the potential of His people today in this day of visitation!**

I believe that the Spirit of God is "setting us up" for the final harvest so that we can properly facilitate His moving upon the face of the earth and adequately accommodate Father's ingathering. Get ready, for this is the hour of *The Final Call.*

Jerry Fitch
New Iberia, Louisiana

Chapter 1

THE MOVE IS ON

Now all these things happened unto them for examples: and they are written for our admonition, upon whom the ends of the world are come.   1 Corinthians 10:11

The move of God is on. The dimension of the Spirit has brought to the Church a freshness that is drawing us closer to our King. There's a sound from Heaven that is being heard by all those who have opened themselves to His call. The invitation is open to all, "Come, he who is hungry, come!"

Church, this is our finest hour, so don't delay. Paul's words to the Church ring clearer than ever, for we are people receiving the taste of the *"world to come"* (Hebrews 6:5), *"upon whom the ends of the world are come."* We are a generation blessed with unprecedented truth, revealed with a heavenly magnitude. Because of it, some have declared this to be the "Joshua Generation," the "Omega Generation," the "Elijah Company," and other names or titles given to the happenings of today. Others have declared this to be the "final outpouring," a renewal. Others say it's revival.

> **Anarchy is at an all-time high, as are riots, wars, racism and hunger, and we see the elements raging uncontrollably!**

Spiritual upheaval permeates our society— both good and bad, and "spiritual hotbeds" are popping up at different areas around the world. They seem to be strategically positioned as though someone (or Someone) had an inside scoop on a well-devised scheme.

The Move Is On

Amidst the hunger of spiritual people, there also seems to be an increase of the spirit of anti-Christ. Anarchy is at an all-time high, as are riots, wars, racism and hunger, and we see the elements raging uncontrollably. Man has risen against his brother, woman against her daughter and friend versus friend.

Economic woes prevail in our society as well. Some are too full, while others go hunger. The same economic roller coaster that takes many up is soon on the downward track, leaving in its wake the disillusionment of entire societies, families and governments. Empty words filled with empty promises leave people feeling the same—empty.

Is this the final call, a renewal or revival? Are we really the "Joshua Generation," or the "Elijah Company?" Is it Pentecost or Tabernacles? Is our laughter holy, our falling spiritual and our visions heavenly? Are we a generation of implementation or transformation? Is the call inward or upward?

My friend, I submit to you that it is not an either/or situation; it is all of the above and then some! Yes, we are the Joshua generation, the Elijah company and every other known and even unknown title that can be used. We *are* experiencing renewal with subsequent revival to follow.

Please hear what I am about to say: We are in the beginning stages of the greatest move of God this planet has ever experienced. As powerful and refreshing as the present moving of the Spirit is, it is still just the beginning. Not only is it just the beginning; what is to come will encompass a certain dimension of each of the past dealings of God with man. We are soon to experience what God meant when He spoke of the former rain and the latter rain combined.

> **We are in the beginning stages of the greatest move of God this planet has ever experienced!**

We must have this understanding if we are to mature in this day. Our God is not just a "Joshua God," or an "Elijah God." He is God of all, and this God will rain Himself upon His people with each and every dimension of history—as we allow Him to do it. Some will enter in and receive the "double-portion" promise of the sixth-day man. Others will be satisfied for the spiritual high they have received and go no further. But, friend, unless we totally open ourselves to the fullness of the plan of God, we will fall drastically short of His greatness.

> **We must have this understanding if we are to mature in this day!**

There is a group of people in Father's earth today who are determined to receive all that He has intended for His children. They will truly be the witnesses that His Word speaks about. They will fulfill the prophecy of Christ Himself that speaks of a people who will usher in the seventh day. What is happening now is the beginning of what must come on the day following, so that the culmination, the perfection of the Bride will be manifested.

The harvesting of the earth is being prepared by God now through the preparation of His people. This is what Paul was speaking about when he mentioned the *"dispensation of the fulness of times"* (Ephesians 1:10). He wasn't speaking of an epoch or a period; rather, he spoke of an arrangement by God. This present move of the Spirit is God-arranged, God-inspired and God-administered! Not only will man not stop it; he can't!

> **What is happening now is the beginning of what must come on the day following, so that the culmination, the perfection of the Bride will be manifested!**

Along with this powerful display of God will come an onslaught of antagonists and criticisms. The critics are coming out by the droves, denying what they cannot understand

and refuse to experience. Imagine the pride and arrogance of these who feel that because they have not experienced a thing or don't understand it, they must deny it or disclaim it as "ungodly" or even "demonic." These have the nerve to believe God won't or can't do something that they don't understand or agree with.

Many of these critics come with a facade of scriptural authority, even though they do not know the spirit of the Scriptures they espouse. They go beyond the boundaries set in the Scriptures and, at the same time, deny the realm of the supernatural. In their ignorance, they declare that God can, but He probably won't. Many will be caught up in this religious mind-set that is causing the faith of many to falter. My friend, do not get caught up in this web of deceit.

> **Many of these critics come with a facade of scriptural authority, even though they do not know the spirit of the Scriptures they espouse!**

I might add that since men cannot understand what God is doing, that could be proof enough that it is God. He doesn't need my approval nor yours to be God. He just does what He wants regardless of what I may or may not feel or think about it. That is what makes Him God. He doesn't need our approval to accomplish His will.

This generation is filled with many questions, and there are few answers. Our government is at its end, our economy is threatened, our judicial system is becoming more and more biased. Education has never been more available, and yet it is not well received. So late in the game, we are still struggling with segregation. Our problems are educational, religious, social, economical and racial, and the list of them is long. What will be the solution? When will all these issues be answered? Is there an answer?

In this book, I want to make a conscious effort to answer, at least to some degree, three important questions:

"Where are we?"
"What's happening?" and
"What's coming next?"

I believe that these three questions pervade every aspect of our society, and there are few answers. I certainly don't pretend to have all the answers either, but I do know what the Lord has spoken to my heart through His Word and by His Spirit. Therefore, I encourage you to lend yourself to the message of the coming pages, and know beyond any doubt that you are on a journey.

> **The road you take will determine your journey's end. You can either take the way of the critic and receive a critic's reward, or you can venture into the realms of God!**

The road you take will determine your journey's end. You can either take the way of the critic and receive a critic's reward, or you can venture into the realms of God, perhaps unknown, but of God nonetheless, and enter into His design and purpose for His creation that is reserved for those *"upon whom the ends of the world are come."* This is *The Final Call*.

Chapter 2

WHERE ARE WE?

And in that day seven women shall take hold of one man, saying, We will eat our own bread, and wear our own apparel: only let us be called by thy name, to take away our reproach. In that day shall the branch of the LORD be beautiful and glorious, and the fruit of the earth shall be excellent and comely for them that are escaped of Israel. And it shall come to pass, that he that is left in Zion, and he that remaineth in Jerusalem, shall be called holy, even every one that is written among the living in Jerusalem: when the LORD shall have washed away the filth of the daughters of Zion, and shall have purged the blood of Jerusalem from the midst thereof by

the spirit of judgment, and by the spirit of
burning.   Isaiah 4:1-4

Our first important question is *Where Are We*? As we begin to probe for an understanding of this question, I believe it is imperative to make a few statements of facts first. I will be speaking generally concerning the issues that we face here in our nation today. For a more in-depth study in these areas, there are many resources available for the serious student.

It is of the utmost importance that an open mind always be present during such a discussion. There is the potential of some getting upset at some of things written, and to some degree, that may be good. If you become upset to the point of changing, then the means will justify the end.

> **If you become upset to the point of changing, then the means will justify the end!**

As a point of interest, let me say that I am not a pessimist; I am totally optimistic concerning this nation and its future. Yet I will not be like the proverbial ostrich that hides its head in the sand, refusing to acknowledge the current condition of the nation. Until and unless America returns to the God of Israel, this nation will continue to get worse. Yes, worse than it is today.

> **Until and unless the church returns to the God of the Bible, she will not and cannot serve a redemptive value to our society!**

It is also notable to recognize that until and unless the church returns to the God of the Bible, she *will not* and *cannot* serve a redemptive value to our society. She will be nothing more than a religious mausoleum of past achievements filled with dead men's bones.

Although we are beginning to see pockets of renewal happening around this country today, for the most part, the move of God is attacked by narrow-minded, self-promoting, self-seeking ministers. Fearful of what they cannot understand, they go about denying God's ability to do whatever He chooses.

Is it possible that history has taught us nothing? One person said, "History has taught us that history has taught us nothing." Is that what is happening again? Must we go around the same mountain again and again? Rather than having the power of God, we choose a *"form of godliness,"* while *"denying the power thereof"* (2 Timothy 3:5).

I think this would be a good place to remind the religious community of today of the Charismatic Movement, and for the older generations, the Latter Day Movement. Remember how offensive these moves seemed to many in the Christian community at the time? Remember how many souls were brought to the saving knowledge of Christ, while the church as a whole denied the authenticity of these movements and even refused to accept their converts?

I am sure that Saul of Tarsus could relate to what is happening today. Are we to allow another Woodstock to take place? Come on, Church, smarten up. God is bigger than you or I.

> **There are still millions of people alive today who are determined to be a part of God's greatest happenings on earth!**

There are still millions of people alive today who are determined to be a part of God's greatest happenings on earth. I am one of them. Are you? We have settled in our hearts and resolved in our lives that He is God, and since He is God, He can do whatever, wherever, to whomever and whenever He chooses. And, friend, you can believe that He will do just that.

So, as we begin to study the question, "Where Are We?" don't get discouraged. At the same time, don't deny the truth either. Things will not end the way they now seem. Read the end of the Book, and you will be encouraged to continue with God.

> **Israel, at the time, was under the judgment of God, and there is judgment for any nation that is not in God's order!**

So, America, Where are we? Our text from Isaiah 4 (it might be wise to read chapter 3 as well) brings us to a time in Israel's history when they were out of the order and structure of God. Not only were they out of His divine pattern, living as they pleased, they were faced with judgments that had no solution to them and were seeking answers outside of God. In time, their confusion led them to seek solutions from wrong sources, therefore multiplying the chaos. Israel, at the time, was under the judgment of God, and there is judgment for any nation that is not in God's order.

America, where are we? As I studied this text in Isaiah and noticed that Israel was under the judgment of God, I saw that we can parallel the perils they faced as a result with what is happening in America today and can conclude only one thing: America is also under the judgment of God.

THINK ABOUT THESE POINTS:

In Isaiah 3:1, the prophet spoke of a time when there was no bread, no water, no life-giving substance. America's welfare system is bankrupt and is constantly under attack. We must seriously question ourselves as to what is going to happen to the welfare system of this country if our present politicians have their way. The homeless are dramatically growing in number daily, as are the hungry and the destitute. At the same time, our $22.03 trillion budget deficit continues to grow daily, and cuts are being made to try to offset this monster. Well, guess where the first cuts are being made. That's right, to our welfare system.

It has been projected by leading economists that the Social Security System will run out of money within the next fifteen years, if not sooner. Medicare, Medicaid, our food stamp programs, and other government sponsorships are all being threatened by bankruptcy or of being severely cut. America, where are we?

> **It has been projected by leading economists that the Social Security System will run out of money within the next fifteen years, if not sooner!**

In Isaiah 3:2, the prophet spoke of a missing voice, of the lack of a warrior spirit. The mighty man, he said, was gone. It seems to me that today all too often the voice of the accuser is being heard, while the voice of God's leaders are being given a deaf ear. Many woes produce many voices. Often the voice of the accuser cries louder than the voice of the needy.

A story was related to me once concerning a man whose house was being burned to the ground. The man escaped the fiery trap without harm, but his baby was still inside in that inferno. The child cried, and that cry caught his father's attention. The firemen tried to prevent the father from entering the house, but to no avail. He would not listen.

As that father entered the burning house, the blaze encompassed him, and everyone was sure that he would not make it back out alive. Then, not very long after the father entered the house, out from the midst of the blazes came a man running with a bundle in his hand. It was the father, and he had his child safely wrapped in his arms.

When someone asked the man why he had not heeded the authorities who warned him not to go back into the house, he answered, "The cry of my child was louder than the cry of those who told me not to go back in there."

> **"The cry of my child was louder than the cry of those who told me not to go back in there!"**

Where is the voice of the mighty man, the judge, the prudent one? Are we going to allow the cry of the critic to be greater than the cry of the needy? Or will we finally surrender to the voice of the prophet and heed God's call? Will the cry of the critic drown out the cry of the needy? America, where are we?

Isaiah 3:4 is very plain; the children had started to rule. This judgement is not hard to discern in the America of today. Too often children rule our streets with weapons that are so sophisticated that only trained personnel have the knowledge to operate them. Still, our children not only have access to these high-tech weapons; they have the knowledge to use them. And, using them, they rule our streets with fear. The result is that innocent people tremble each time they have to leave their homes.

Where Are We?

I'm not just talking about the large cities anymore; this atrocity has hit rural America as well. Street gangs rule with violence and prey upon the innocent with little fear of consequence. In fact, they even boast about what they do on national television.

> **Too often children rule our streets with weapons that are so sophisticated that only trained personnel have the knowledge to operate them!**

One national talk show had gang members as their "guests," and they spoke openly of the killings they had done with no remorse and then bragged about their intention to do more killings. They boldly stated that there was nothing the law could do about it. Sad to say, they appear to be right.

What can we say about the lawlessness that abounds in our public schools today? Teachers are being shot because their students don't like having to do homework. Metal detectors are being placed in the entrance to schools because children and young people are bringing weapons to school—guns, knives and other weapons. This is happening across the nation.

> **What can we say about the lawlessness that abounds in our public schools today?**

What about our homes? They were intended to be a place of solace, a place of escape from all fear and dread? May I submit to you that the lack of respect in our world today concerning authority is first of all seen in our homes? If children don't respect their parents, do you think for one minute that they will respect the law, their teachers, or any other authority figure? I think not. Children now rule our homes, and that rule extends far beyond the home.

Where Are We?

There are actual laws that now prohibit the discipline of children, and then there are laws that punish parents when their children become law-breakers. To me, something seems terribly wrong with that combination. Parents are afraid to discipline their children for fear of being accused of child abuse, and, therefore, that child can run rampant over their parents. America, where are we?

> **If children don't respect their parents, do you think for one minute that they will respect the law, their teachers, or any other authority figure?**

Isaiah 3:5 speaks about people being oppressed by one another and children behaving proudly against the ancient (the elderly). This is not hard to see today. It is neighbor against neighbor. The very word, *neighbor*, should signify friendliness, but that has changed.

And what about children behaving proudly against the elderly? You cannot pick up a newspaper today without seeing where a child has killed an adult. It is children killing parents, children killing authority figures, children killing just for the sake of killing. America, where are we?

> **America is in desperate need of qualified leadership today!**

Isaiah 3:6 speaks of the need for leadership, but no one responds. America is in desperate need of qualified leadership today. Notice I prefaced that with the word *qualified*. And, again, none respond. The intense interrogations that individuals go through to hold a public office is nothing more than a sham.

Today, honest, upright citizens are denied public office because of some indiscretion in their past. I believe that integrity is vital to leadership, but if someone has made a mistake in the past and has since rectified it, we need to let it die.

We have all made mistakes that should keep us from being anything, but God forgives. What about us? There is the distinct possibility that people who never get the chance to rule because of something from their past certainly could do no worse than those who do rule. When none of the qualified come forward, that leaves the unqualified to rule. Do you disqualify someone for past failures? God doesn't, so why should we.? Calvary is God's answer for past failures. America, where are we?

> **Isaiah 3:8 indicates that God was being forgotten in ancient Israel, and He is all but forgotten in America today!**

Isaiah 3:8 indicates that God was being forgotten in ancient Israel, and He is all but forgotten in America today. Laws are being enacted almost daily that are clearly against God and His people. This nation, founded upon freedom of worship, is now removing God from every public place. Our houses of worship are constantly under the scrutiny of the Internal Revenue Service. Let me say that accountability is good, but when you are being scrutinized for the sole purpose of removing God from the land, something has to change.

The separation of church and state is no more than a cliché used by lawmakers for their own agendas. Nativity scenes are being outlawed because of a few protesters, while humanism pervades the textbooks used in our public schools and even permeates the very fabric of our society through laws and the opinions of the powerful. America, where are we?

Isaiah 3:9 declares, *"The shew of their countenance doth witness against them; and they declare their sin as Sodom, they hide it not."* Today, here in America, there is open sin and rebellion against God with no shame attached to it. People openly admit to homosexuality, lesbianism and all other forms of perversion, and they do it without feeling or showing any remorse or shame whatsoever. In fact, their faces beam with pride for their sin, and they could care less if anyone is adversely affected by it.

> **Today, here in America, there is open sin and rebellion against God with no shame attached to it!**

When homosexuals first began "coming out of the closet," people were amazed, surprised and baffled. Now, however, there doesn't even seem to be a closet to come out of. The closet has been turned inside out. But, don't be surprised when more sin comes out of the closet and becomes mainstream.

God's Word is very clear about this particular sin. Call it what you will; God still calls it sin! The audacity of these people, trying to convince us that all they want is to be treated like everyone else. That is one of the greatest lies that Hell has concocted over the recent years of this "openness." The fact is that they are *not* like everyone else.

According to the Word of God, those who do these things have *"a reprobate mind"* and have been given over by God because *"they did not like to retain God in their knowledge"* (Romans 1:28). This kind of perversion is a direct judgment upon a nation that rejects God. For a greater understanding of these truths, read Romans 1. Verse 32 is especially powerful:

> *Who knowing the judgment of God, that they which commit such things are worthy of death, not only do the same, but have pleasure in them that do them.*
>
> Romans 1:32

This kind of perversion is a direct judgment upon a nation that rejects God!

Where Are We?

America, where are we?

Isaiah 3:12 shows that women ruling is another sign of judgment. The verse speaks also of the tyranny of youth, and I have already written about that. Allow me to add that any nation that is under the oppression of its future (its youth) is in big trouble.

Again, women ruling is a direct sign of God's judgment upon a nation. I didn't say it, God did. I'm just repeating what He said. Equal Rights, Women's Lib and all the other groups that have formed specifically for the emasculation of man are thriving, and that is a direct signal that our nation is under judgment.

"Well, don't you think that a woman can do
everything that a man can do?"
"Shouldn't a woman get equal pay
for equal work?"
"Aren't we all created equal?"

These questions and many others like them have fogged the hidden agenda of these dangerous women's groups. No, we are not created equal.

> **These questions and many others like them have fogged the hidden agenda of these dangerous women's groups.**

"Shouldn't a woman have power over her own body?"

The bombardment of deceptive arguments to distract from the real spirit behind these demonic movements goes on and on.

"Well, a woman can do anything a man can do." Well maybe, but men can't do what women can do. For example, men cannot abort (murder) 1.5 million unborn children a year, like women do. And these statistics are only of the reported abortions. I am sure that this figure could potentially double if all abortions were reported. Women ruling has caused multiple millions of murders in this nation, but this hasn't gone unnoticed. God keeps very good records!

God keeps very good records!

What is behind these movements? It is Satan's plan to try to destroy God's order for the home, the nation and the church. America, where are we?

Isaiah 3:16-26 speaks of sexual promiscuity. The sexual revolution may have been declared in the 1960s and 70s, but it has now reached full bloom. Illicit sex ravishes this nation like nothing else could. The desecration of our wedding vows and, with it, the desecration of God's order has become so open and visible that no one can deny it. In fact, it seems to be "posh" to do anything contrary to the Word of God when it comes to sex.

Let me say to you: such actions are not without their consequences. No nation with immorality at an all-time high as it is in this nation can go unpunished.

Now, instead of teaching abstinence, our government is passing out free condoms to our children. Instead of putting the lid on sexual sin, the entire jar has now been poured out. The mentality of the world and our leaders is to control this destructive craving that is literally wiping out entire cities. Friend, you don't control an epidemic; it must be conquered!

> **There is only one answer to the epidemic that is raping our nation, and that is for the nation to turn back to Jehovah God and repents of its sins and be cleansed by the blood of the Lamb!**

AIDS is an epidemic that has literally taken over our nation. The latest statistic is that one out of every four teenagers is infected with the virus that causes AIDS. The leading cause of death of those between the ages of eighteen and twenty today is AIDS.

Can I say to you that it is not a virus that causes AIDS? It is sexual promiscuity, illicit sex and drug abuse that causes AIDS! Sin causes

AIDS! And it is time that our government discovered the fact that you cannot legislate AIDS away! You cannot vote it out! You cannot control it! There is only one answer to the epidemic that is raping our nation, and that is for the nation to turn back to Jehovah God and repents of its sins and be cleansed by the blood of the Lamb!

But sexual promiscuity is intoxicating, and our nation is drunk on it.

Consider, if you will, for a moment, what AIDS stands for:

A-Acquired. AIDS is something that you acquire. You don't just get AIDS, you have to make a conscious effort to acquire it. AIDS doesn't just happen. No, you have to find it. It is a conscious decision one makes to get AIDS. AIDS is not even a mistake; it is a decision. (I will explain what I mean by this on the following pages.

I-Immunity. Our body has been designed with a system that protects it from foreign substances. It is called the immune system. Once AIDS enters the system, there is no more immunity to fight it. In fact, the body then becomes immune to any substance that tries to conquer the AIDS virus. But, once again, this didn't just happen. It's an *acquired* immunity. The body's system cannot ward off this deadly virus. This virus is itself immune to seemingly anything and everything.

> **Once AIDS enters the system, there is no more immunity to fight it!**

D-Deficiency. There is a lack of whatever is needed in the body to fight the AIDS virus. Our bodies were not created to acquire AIDS, but now there is a deficiency there.

At this point, I must inject this: homosexuality, lesbianism, and all other sorts of perverted sex are nothing more than an invitation for this deadly disease that is killing multiple millions of people worldwide (including millions of Americans). It comes to destroy you, but it comes at your request.

If a man wants to justify his sexual promiscuity, than his reward is AIDS. The only protection against this deadly sin is godly living and nothing else! Your condoms won't do it, your motto's won't do it, your government programs won't do it, your safe sex won't do it, and certainly your support groups (which are often nothing more than a glorified pity party) won't do it. The only safeguard from AIDS is morality, and this nation has plunged headlong into immorality and is paying the piper for it!

> **The only protection against this deadly sin is godly living and nothing else!**

Call your psychic hot-line and see if they can help you. Call your sex hot-line and see if they will come to your rescue. No, sir, you're all alone with this sin that is killing you. Immorality is destroying the very fabric that has made this nation great.

Your President, attorney general and senators and congressman who supported your sexual "rights" are nowhere to be found when you are on your death bed, anguishing in unrelenting pain. But it need not be. Come to Jesus, and let godliness once again prevail in your life!

Come to Jesus, and let godliness once again prevail in your life!

S-Syndrome. A syndrome is "a group of signs and symptoms that occur together and characterize a particular abnormality." It is not normal to have AIDS. This disease is out of the realm of normalcy. Just because a friend has acquired the virus, just because you know someone who has the virus, just because the world's superstars have the virus doesn't make it normal. The normal ones are the ones who do *not* have AIDS. They, by the way, are also the smart ones!

Let me insert this note: there are some innocent victims today who are suffering unjustly because of the "rights" of others who have AIDS. Through blood transfusions or a mishap at the dentist's or doctor's office, this virus is sometimes being transmitted to innocent people. If there is to be any legislation concerning AIDS, let it be that your doctor, dentist or any other person who is having close contact with you, must disclose in advance if they are infected with this virus. That kind of legislation should protect the innocent and put the rights where they belong—with innocent people.

> **If there is to be any legislation concerning AIDS, let it be that your doctor, dentist or any other person who is having close contact with you, must disclose in advance if they are infected with this virus!**

To those who have been unjustly infected, my prayers are with you, and I will stand with you in the gap for a miracle from God. God bless you.

Sin in our personal lives is like AIDS in the sense that a "bucket" of sin will not just suddenly fall upon you. Sin is **A**cquired in that it can either be refused or accepted. It is a conscious decision made on the part of a person to accept sin and then continue in sin. And the deeper problem is that sin will always affect our spiritual **I**mmunity system. If sin is condoned in our lives, it will continue to develop until it eventually destroys our spirituality. It becomes easier and easier to live with that sin, and then to make room for other sins to enter and develop. Un-repented sin causes **D**eficiency in our spirit. As God's children, our spirit needs strength, not something that will diminish our spirit further. A weak spirit is an abnormality, a **S**yndrone. Sin diminishes us, but righteousness exalts us.

Again, our nation is drunken with uncontrollable sexual desires that are literally ripping the nation apart. America, where are we?

Where Are We?

I want to declare that anytime you see these things happening in a nation, there is only one thing you can conclude: that nation is under the judgment of God. Israel was under God's judgment, and these were the evidences. America, with these sign, it is clear that we, too, are under God's judgment. If you will study this chapter in Isaiah in detail, you will find that I was not exhaustive in its descriptions. I only used these few verses to support my statement of this nation's judgment.

I want to also declare that anytime you see any of these signs prevailing and remaining in the church, that church will soon be under the judgment of God as well, and it cannot be long before the life of God is gone out of it, and the people have perished or sought another place where God's life reigns.

> **Israel was under God's judgment, and these were the evidences!**

> **My feeling is that Isaiah was speaking about what we now commonly call "a Jezebel spirit!"**

Yes, it is possible for the church to be under God's judgment. Peter wrote:

> *For the time is come that judgment must begin at the house of God: and if it first begin at us, what shall the end be of them that obey not the gospel of God?*   1 Peter 4:17

God's purpose in judgment is always redemptive, not destructive. It only becomes destructive when we do not heed His warnings.

Possibly the clearest sign recorded in Isaiah 3 that a church is under judgment is found in verse 12:

> *... women rule over them. O my people, they which lead thee cause thee to err, and destroy the way of thy paths.*

Where Are We?

My feeling is that Isaiah was speaking about what we now commonly call "a Jezebel spirit." There is a big difference with women in authority and women ruling. God has a place, according to the Scriptures, where qualified women are to be in authority. That is not the issue we are addressing.

God has much to say about a Jezebel ruling, and what He has to say shows us that this is a sign of His judgment. Therefore, let us examine this matter of a Jezebel spirit and you can decide if it is operating in the church you attend.

So, what is a "Jezebel spirit?" This spirit is present when a person tries to manipulate and/or control a person of authority over

> **The spirit of Jezebel can be identified in our society and churches as the source of obsessive sensuality, uncontrollable witchcraft and total disregard for male authority!**

them. This name Jezebel can be translated, and it means "without cohabitation." This simply means that she will not co-habit with or live together with anyone she cannot control and dominate. That is how this spirit works, through the desire to dominate others.

> **Wherever the opportunity presents itself for control, the spirit of Jezebel will certainly respond!**

The spirit of Jezebel can be identified in our society and churches as the source of obsessive sensuality, uncontrollable witchcraft and total disregard for male authority. It is an independent spirit that strives for preeminence and total control. The deceptiveness of the spirit is that, while Jezebel is associated with every means of sexual perversion, the real target behind this spirit is always control.

Where Are We?

The spirit of Jezebel is the spirit of witchcraft. *Witchcraft* means "to smite with the eyes." Witchcraft is manifested in three ways:

1). Manipulation,
2). Intimidation and
3). Domination.

According to Revelation 2:19-29, this spirit was present, sitting in the church of Thyatira nearly two thousand years ago. Although the spirit of Jezebel has been around much longer than that, I want you to notice where it lodged—in the church.

This spirit will rule over entire countries, states, provinces, cities, towns, townships, churches, homes and governments. Wherever the opportunity presents itself for control, the spirit of Jezebel will certainly respond.

Having been involved in full-time Christian ministry now for more than forty years, I have had the opportunity to see this spirit manifest itself on many occasions and in many different ways. Following are some of my personal observations concerning the manifestations of the spirit of Jezebel:

> **The spirit of Jezebel promotes itself in the eyes of others to lure them away from God-appointed leadership!**

1. The spirit of Jezebel pretends to want true Christian doctrine, while, all along, it only seeks to utilize God's Word to its own fleshly desires. When confronted with truth, it claims that it is under attack for being "so spiritual."

2. The spirit of Jezebel promotes itself in the eyes of others to lure them away from God-appointed leadership, usually preying on the discontented, the angry or offended and the weak.

3. The spirit of Jezebel belittles male figures, preferring the disposition of women.

4. The spirit of Jezebel is always sowing seeds of discord, to bring division in the Body. It will often serve as an instigator, stirring up discord, then pulling away, leaving someone else to assume the responsibility or blame for the division.

> **The husband will relinquish his role in the home, preferring "peace" rather than always arguing with his wife!**

5. Unless the spirit of Jezebel is totally removed, cast down or cast out, it will never totally release the area that it is trying to control. Instead, it will constantly bombard certain places, people and works until either the spirit is conquered or the people, places and/or works are destroyed. Be not deceived, the spirit of Jezebel is a very destructive and deadly spirit.

6. The spirit of Jezebel in a woman will usually choose to marry and dominate a

weaker husband. The husband will relinquish his role in the home, preferring "peace" rather than always arguing with his wife. This is one way domination is demonstrated.

> **The Jezebel spirit will try to act as a "spiritual thermometer," gauging the services as to their "anointedness" or godliness or lack thereof!**

The spirit of Jezebel manipulates the home by:

- Withholding sex
- Throwing fits of rage
- Pouting
- Embarrassing the husband in public places
- Excessive spending to pacify the rage

The spirit of Jezebel manipulates the church by:

1. Convincing people that they (the people) should have "more say so" in the church.

2. Controlling the pastor by befriending his wife. By befriending the wife, this spirit can plant in her negative thoughts, thus belittling and degrading the pastor and/ or his wife. For example, "If you would only pray more, ..." Let me also add that this spirit will not only attach itself to the pastor's wife, but to any person in leader-ship position—but especially the pastor's wife.

3. The Jezebel spirit will use fear tactics. For example, it will say something like this, "God showed me that if the church doesn't do <u>this or that</u>, then He will pour His wrath upon it."

4. The Jezebel spirit will try to act as a "spiri-tual thermometer," gauging the services as to their "anointedness" or godliness or lack thereof. When someone says, "Wasn't that a great service?" the Jezebel spirit will answer something like, "Well, yes, but ... ."

> **The Jezebel spirit will even allow itself to remain dormant for a period of time in order for the individual to use his or her talents to get into a position of leadership or authority where they can then better control things!**

5. The Jezebel spirit will always be "clickish," having its own little group and always feeding them its doctrine. Even more so, this spirit will feed off of the people of the group, for they are convinced that this person is very spiritual and so right about everything that they, unconsciously or not, supply this spirit nourishment to continue to dominate and control. The Jezebel spirit needs to continually receives this type of support from her following, and usually gets it.

6. The Jezebel spirit will even allow itself to remain dormant for a period of time in order for the individual to use his or her talents to get into a position of leadership or authority where they can then better control things. Frightening, isn't it?

The wife will not be able to have friends, even women friends, nor, in extreme cases, will she even be allowed to go outside!

In continuation of point #6, I might add that, if it is not cast out, the spirit of Jezebel will be transferred to the children. It will then manifest in the young ladies by:

1. The girls will seek husbands just like their fathers, i.e. weak, and easily controlled.

This spirit will be manifested in young men by:

1. They will be obsessed with the total domination and control of their wives, to the point that they will literally take away the wife's personality and replace it with their own. This is done through fear and excessive possession. The wife will not be able to have friends, even women friends, nor, in extreme cases, will she even be allowed to go outside. The husband will be extremely and irrationally jealous.

2. When the Jezebel spirit is in boys, that young man will seek a woman like his mother (because of the role model he had in the home). Seeking a wife like his mother, he then submits himself again to that spirit, only this time it is in his wife. Because he had no proper role model from his father, this

God has given us power over this spirit!

allows the wicked cycle to continue. A recent survey has noted that a boy who has a domineering mother and a father who allows this to happen is more likely to have homosexual tendencies or even become a homosexual. Can we conclude that a Jezebel spirit could be the cause, or at least, one of the causes of homosexuality in both boys and men and girls and women?

> **I can honestly say that through "much tribulation" we have entered the Kingdom (Acts 14:12)!**

The Jezebel spirit will divide churches into factions and then leave if it cannot control things, leaving the church with the influence of that spirit.

A Jezebel spirit will literally bewitch those who follow it (remember that the Jezebel spirit is the spirit of witchcraft), even though time after time their own works and words prove that the individual carrying this spirit is a liar.

When you examine the destruction and deceptiveness of this spirit, it almost leaves you feeling helpless. But please understand that God has given us power over this spirit. The spirit of Jezebel cannot, I repeat, *cannot* operate unless there is an Ahab present.

For every Jezebel there must be an Ahab, but praise God, for every Ahab there is an Elijah! God is once again raising up the spirit of Elijah in His Church to bring an end to this evil, divisive and destructive spirit!

Looking back on the chapter now and our context from Isaiah 3 and 4, all of these signs are a curse to a people who have forsaken God! So, Church, where are we?

I have shown you what happens to a community, Christian or otherwise, that is outside the blessing and order of God. Now let me tell you where we are today. I can honestly say that through *"much tribulation"* we have entered the Kingdom (Acts 14:12). We have dealt with the anarchy of the church, God has brought down the proud and the boastful, the disobedient and the rebellious, and He has raised up a group of people who refuse to be called the son of Pharaoh's daughter (see Hebrews 11:24)!

Isaiah 3:13 says:

> *The* L*ORD* *standeth up to plead, and standeth to judge the people.*

My friend, the Righteous Judge is standing and His verdict is pending. Where are we? We are properly positioned for the greatest harvest of all time. God has restored order to the Church, we have decided to choose Him and live, and the "redeemed nation," the Church, will become the only safety in our society!

Let's examine what God says about His Church:

1. In Genesis 28:16-19, Jacob found himself at Bethel. *Bethel* means "the house of God," and, in this context, the "house of God" is called *"the gate of heaven."* This is God's way

to eternity, His Church in proper order, under His direction and the influence of the Holy Spirit.

It is in the House of God that visions of God are manifested. Outside that order, the visions are blurred and out of sorts, but in the House of God, you see clearly the heartbeat of God.

I must declare to you, at this point, that if you are not part of a local church that is ministering in the power of His might, if you are not part of a local church that preaches the uncompromising, unadulterated Word of God, then get to one that is! Anything else is death. Life is in the Word of God! Notice that I didn't say "religion." I say, rather, a

> **If you are not part of a local church that preaches the uncompromising, unadulterated Word of God, then get to one that is!**

church that is doing the will of God and preaching the Word of God. That, by God's choice, is *"the gate to heaven."*

Here's an interesting and important statistic worth noting concerning what God's Word says about the local church: Did you know that out of the one hundred and fourteen times the word *church* is mentioned or alluded to in the New Testament, that ninety percent or one hundred and two of those times, it is referring to a set group of people in a particular geographical location? This is the local church. And how important is

> **This is the local church. And how important is it? It is "the house of God," and "the gate of heaven." It is the way that God has chosen to direct people to eternity with Him through Jesus Christ!**

it? It is *"the house of God,"* and *"the gate of heaven."* It is the way that God has chosen to direct people to eternity with Him through Jesus Christ.

2. Next, let us examine 2 Chronicles 20:9:

> *If, when evil cometh upon us, as the sword, judgment, or pestilence, or famine, we stand before this house, and in thy presence, (for thy name is in this house,) and cry unto thee in our affliction, then thou wilt hear and help.*

People are always searching for the answers to what troubles them in life. They are always looking but often searching in all the wrong places. I have good news for all who are searching with an honest and open heart. Your answer is found in the House of God. The church that is in the order of God has the answer for all of life's troubles. Of course, His name is Jesus.

Notice what this text declares. First of all, it once again directs people who are searching to the right direction for their answer, the House of God. Next, the text declares that God's presence is there, and His name is there. Friend, the Church is not *your* church. It does not belong to a board, a committees, a denomination, or to any special interest group. It is not the sole property of either the rich or the poor. It doesn't even belong to a preacher. It belongs to God! It is His Church and only His Church, and this is the Church the gates of Hell will not

> **As we gather together, in a specific geographical location, we fulfill His order for the Church!**

prevail against (see Matthew 16:18)! That, my friend, is the attribute only of the true Church. "*The gates of hell will not prevail against it.*"

This does not mean that there won't be attacks; it just means that the attacks won't succeed! We are God's purchased possession. He has put His name upon us. We are His

Church, and as we gather together, in a specific geographical location, we fulfill His order for *the* Church.

Not only is His name there; His presence is there also. I have stood in the presence of some great people in some great places and witnessed some great events in my life, but none can compare with being in the presence of the Lord. His Word declares that when we come to His House and stand in His presence, then will He hear us and help us. Amen!

Brother or Sister, your answer is in the House of the Lord. Neighbor, your answer is in the House of the Lord. Preacher, your answer is in the House!

> **The Church lays the foundation through the apostles and prophets, with Jesus Christ Himself being the Chief Cornerstone (see Ephesians 2:20)!**

3. In 1 Timothy 3:15, Paul made an interesting analogy:

> *But if I tarry long, that thou mayest know how thou oughtest to behave thyself in the house of God, which is the church of the living God, the pillar and ground of the truth.*

Here Paul states that the Church is *"the pillar and ground of truth."* Simply put, the Church in God's order is where the truth is. That church is proper soil for planting and reaping.

A pillar is placed on a proper foundation to support a structure. The Church lays the foundation through the apostles and prophets, with Jesus Christ Himself being the Chief Cornerstone (see Ephesians 2:20). That foundation with that pillar will support the Church of Jesus Christ.

The *"ground"* must be properly prepared so that the foundation will be able to support the building. The Scriptures declares: *"for other foundation can no man lay than that is laid, which is Jesus Christ"* (1 Corinthians

3:11). When the ground has been properly prepared and can support the structure, the results are stability. God says that is where we are!

Although things may seem bleak in some areas, don't give up the faith. Don't lose hope. God's Church will arise and is arising even now in this hour and is becoming, once again, vibrant, viable and vital to this generation, for the harvest is yet before us. As I noted earlier in the book, there are pockets of revival springing up across America, many in obscure places, sometimes with what may seem like the least likely people to lead them, but it is God's choosing. Enter in while the waters are being troubled. America still has hope, because the Church is coming alive in Christ.

Chapter 3

WHAT'S HAPPENING?

Behold, I will do a new thing; now it shall spring forth; shall ye not know it? I will even make a way in the wilderness, and rivers in the desert. Isaiah 43:19

The next question we want to answer in this book is "What's Happening?" In other words, what is the Lord doing in our day and age? Is it a new thing? Or is it just the same thing He has been desiring to accomplish all along?

Mans resistance to the move of God is not new. In fact, history repeatedly shows that man has always had some difficulty coming to grips with the fact that God can do things without his permission.

It has been said that the greatest threat to the present move of God is the prior move of God. That seems to be true. Each past move of God has, in some way, directly affected the present move of God in a negative sense. Yet, God, in all of His wisdom, continues to choose to manifest Himself through man to get His will accomplished. Church fathers, do not throw away what you do not yet understand. Give God the opportunity to show Himself in this generation. He will do it anyway, with or without your cooperation.

> **Each past move of God has, in some way, directly affected the present move of God in a negative sense!**

For many in the Body of Christ, there has been an ever-increasing hunger for God to move. Much prayer has been the result of this hunger, and God is filling us once again. The *status quo* is not enough for these God-seeking,

What's Happening?

Spirit-filled believers, those of us who believe that God means what He says and says what He means. We possess a radical faith, a reckless and abandoned trust that God is still God and will be glorified in the earth. This generation will certainly taste the life of God, and it is to these whom the Lord will appear in His glory.

The psalmist made mention of God's promises for the *"generation to come"* (Psalm 78:4). Paul said the promises were for those *"upon whom the ends of the world is come"* (1 Corinthians 10:11). Is the blessing, then, to be withheld for another generation, another epoch of time? Or is it possible that each and every generation can have opportunity to taste of the world to come?

I, for one, firmly believe that the Word of God is applicable to each and every generation, and that opportunity is before you and me right now. I have decided to taste and see that the Lord is good!

And I am not alone. Multiplied millions of God's children have decided that God is the God of now and are pressing into the fullness of His splendor now. Yesterday is gone, and tomorrow may be too late. As God Himself has said, *"Now is the accepted time!"* (2 Corinthians 6:2).

CONSIDERING PENTECOST

And when the day of Pentecost was fully come, they were all with one accord in one place.   Acts 2:1

What do you think about Pentecost? Is it just a festival that the Jews celebrate, or could it also be something that is pertinent for believers today? What about Pentecost? What is it to believers?

> **To the first-century Christians, Pentecost was monumental. It was everything. It turned things around for them!**

What's Happening?

To the first-century Christians, Pentecost was monumental. It was everything. It turned things around for them. Suddenly they went from despair to elation.

I want to submit to you that the elements that led to the success of that first Pentecost in Jerusalem could have been the promise of Jesus, an expectation on the part of His disciples and some desperation. Desperation? Yes, desperation in the sense of fear because of the hostility of the first-century Jews toward Christ and His followers. That was still in the air. Remember, the Jews had just crucified the Lord Jesus Himself. And they were not about to stop there.

There was also an element of desperation in the early disciples because of a sense of an unfulfilled destiny. Jesus, their hope, had physically died and been buried. Yes, He rose from the dead, appeared to them again and reassured them that the promises were still coming. He spoke particularly of one promise, that He called *"the promise of the Father"*:

And, being assembled together with them, commanded them that they should not depart from Jerusalem, but wait for the promise of the Father, which, saith he, ye have heard of me. Acts 1:4

What was this *"promise of the Father"*? The disciples only knew what Jesus had told them about it, and that wasn't much. And yet this promise was so important to them that, according to Acts 1:1-4, all ministry was now suspended until the promise could be fulfilled. There were to be no miracles, no healings and even no preaching of the Gospel until the promise came!

> **There were to be no miracles, no healings and even no preaching of the Gospel until the promise came!**

They had all heard the same promise. Father God had a gift for each of them. For some, no doubt, this never quite sunk in. Now, out of desperation, they sought God until the promise came.

I have heard it said that desperation is better than despair, and I believe it. These men and women were desperate for God. Jesus' promise led them to have an expectation that something good was coming. What was it? They didn't know for sure. They had no actual knowledge of what was to happen. All they had was an expectation, a trust, because Jesus had given them the promise.

Try to imagine what that must have felt like, waiting for something that Jesus had promised, but having given them no details of what it would be like.

Try to imagine what that must have felt like, waiting for something that Jesus had promised, but having given them no details of what it would be like!

They had no clues at all to enable them to identify the promise when it finally came, just Jesus' words of command that they should *"wait for the promise."*

Yes, He had said one more thing, just before He was taken up into Heaven:

> *But ye shall receive power, after that the Holy Ghost is come upon you: and ye shall be witnesses unto me both in Jerusalem, and in all Judaea, and in Samaria, and unto the uttermost part of the earth.* Act 1:8

So they were going to receive power, but what would that power look like? How would they know when that power from on high had come? What would identify it?

They were going to receive power, but what would that power look like?

Why, do you suppose, Jesus didn't inform these men and women with more details? Is it possible that their deep desire for Christ and for this promised gift could have resulted in the potential to manufacture some manifestation, some prostitution of the real? Personally, I believe that is exactly why Jesus didn't tell them more. In order to maintain the purity of the gift, He simply told them to go and wait, and the promise would come. That was exactly what they did, and it happened. It happened suddenly.

It Happened Suddenly

And when the day of Pentecost was fully come, they were all with one accord in one place. And suddenly there came a sound from heaven as of a rushing mighty wind, and it filled all the house where they were sitting.

Acts 2:1-2

One translation of verse 1 says, *"As the day dawned."* I like that. It speaks of a new opportunity. Yesterday was gone. It was over, with all of its frustrations, fears and inhibitions. Now, a new day was dawning, and with that new day came new opportunities for God's glory. A new day brought new hope, a new freshness. A new day was beginning, and they were all part of it.

Then verse 2 says, *"And suddenly there came a sound from heaven ... ."* Notice the origin of this thing. It came from Heaven. The baptism of the Holy Spirit is God-sent. And, let me say to you, everything that accompanies the baptism of the Holy Spirit is God-sent. Everything!

> **God's suddenlies are always disruptive. They thrust themselves into our lives, disturbing the norm!**

God's suddenlies are always disruptive. They thrust themselves into our lives, disturbing the norm. They never come wrapped up neatly with a bow on top. You never know exactly when they're coming, but because Jesus said they *are* coming, you should always be anticipating them and have the utmost desire to receive them when they do come.

It is in the suddenlies of God that prevailing power arrangements are disrupted and removed, and that is precisely what happened at Pentecost. The Pentecost Festival, which had always captivated a crowd, suddenly lost its attractiveness and its power to captivate the audience. Thousands were now swept out of the previous structure and rituals and were literally captivated by the Life of God manifested through Pentecost!

> **Thousands were now swept out of the previous structure and rituals and were literally captivated by the Life of God manifested through Pentecost!**

"WHAT MEANETH THIS?"

And they were all amazed, and were in doubt, saying one to another, What meaneth this? Acts 2:12

Imagine how the one hundred and twenty believers in the Upper Room must have felt. Suddenly there was a sound from Heaven *"as a rushing mighty wind."* I don't know about you, but that certainly would have gotten my attention.

The Bible doesn't say what these men and women were doing at that exact moment, but we know they were waiting for something. Were they expecting the sound of a rushing mighty wind? I don't think so.

Next, the Bible says:

> *And there appeared unto them cloven tongues like as of fire, and it sat upon each of them.*
> Acts 2:3

That probably wasn't expected either. If I would have seen that, there is no doubt that I would have fainted (under the power of God or otherwise).

Next the Spirit of God entered them, and they *"began to speak with other tongues, as the Spirit gave them utterance"*:

> # Were they expecting the sound of a rushing mighty wind? I don't think so!

And they were all filled with the Holy Ghost, and began to speak with other tongues, as the Spirit gave them utterance.   Acts 2:4

Keep in mind the source of all this. It all came from Heaven. We must all admit that what happened at Pentecost was weird, to say the least. It was definitely outside of the normal routine of everyday life. Let me also add: these manifestations were obvious, not hidden or obscure. It was all very obvious, very different and, ye, very weird.

The response of the people who witnessed it was, *"What meaneth this?"* In today's vernacular, we would say, "What's happening? What's going on? What does this mean?" When that question was asked, *"What meaneth this?,"* Peter stood up to address the crowd.

> **It was all very obvious,
> very different and,
> ye, very weird!**

These were people from many different lands visiting Jerusalem for the feast, and the one hundred and twenty Christian believers had just been speaking the praises of God in their native languages. Now, Peter was about to explain to them what was happening.

That men and women could speak languages they had never studied or learned is an amazing miracle. In the flesh, it is impossible, but because of a powerful impartation of the Holy Spirit, these men and women were able to speak the praises of God in every language represented at that festival. Wow!

> **The mockers present
> that day came to the
> conclusion that these
> people were drunk!**

What's Happening?

The mockers present that day came to the conclusion that these people were drunk (see verse 13). That didn't make sense either because what drunkard suddenly begins to speak a language he has never learned? It doesn't happen.

Acts 2:15-16 records Peter explanation. He said:

> *For these are not drunken, as ye suppose, seeing it is but the third hour of the day. But this is that which was spoken by the prophet Joel.*

What was it that Joel had said?

> *And it shall come to pass in the last days, saith God, I will pour out of my Spirit upon all flesh.*   Acts 2:17

Peter was very specific in his answer about what Joel had prophesied that was now coming to pass in this strange event. Therefore, it would be to our advantage to look at precisely what was foretold.

And it shall come to pass afterward, that I will pour out my spirit upon all flesh; and your sons and your daughters shall prophesy, your old men shall dream dreams, your young men shall see visions: and also upon the servants and upon the handmaids in those days will I pour out my spirit. And I will shew wonders in the heavens and in the earth, blood, and fire, and pillars of smoke. The sun shall be turned into darkness, and the moon into blood, before the great and terrible day of the LORD come. And it shall come to pass, that whosoever shall call on the name of the LORD shall be delivered: for in mount Zion and in Jerusalem shall be deliverance, as the LORD hath said, and in the remnant whom the LORD shall call. Joel 2:28-32

Take a close look at these verses. Do you find any mention of a rushing, mighty wind, of tongues of fire sitting upon each of them, of men and women being drunk without having taken anything to cause it and then being able to speak strange languages?

Do you find any mention of a rushing, mighty wind, of tongues of fire sitting upon each of them, of men and women being drunk without having taken anything to cause it and then being able to speak strange languages?

What made the observers at Pentecost say that the disciples of Jesus were drunk in the first place? Did they stagger like drunken men? Did they fall down, like drunken people often do? Joel had made no mention of any of this, and yet Peter had said emphatically, *"This is that which was spoken by the prophet Joel."* This caused the crowd to be amazed and to ask, *"What meaneth this?"* or What's happening?"

THE PRESENT MOVE OF GOD

The present move of God is under attack by many who feel, for some reason or another, that God cannot do anything they cannot understand or anything that is not written in the Bible. Let me say, first of all, God is the God ocer His Word. I believe in the inerrant Word of God. That makes me smarter than some already. I also believe that, since God is God, He can do whatever He chooses, and He can do it without asking our permission. To try to limit God under the facade of protecting His integrity will not stop Him from doing what He has decided to do. Just because there are some manifestations occurring today that are not written in the Bible, we must be careful in judging what is God and what isn't.

> **What made the observers at Pentecost say that the disciples of Jesus were drunk in the first place?**

Take careful note again that the drunkenness, the staggering and falling down and the speaking in tongues were not mentioned in Joel's prophecy, yet Peter emphatically linked these manifestations with that prophecy. Now either God can do things that are not mentioned in His Word, or there is a contradiction in the Scriptures. I submit that God can do whatever He chooses and however He chooses.

> **I submit that God can do whatever He chooses and however He chooses!**

Yes, I believe in the inerrancy of the Scriptures. But let's not deny what we don't yet understand. Be discerning by the Spirit, but do not be judgmental in the flesh.

My Pentecostal brethren will agree with me when I say that speaking in tongues is for today, and they will be unwavering in their efforts to defend what *they* have experienced as being from God. Yet, I have other friends who do not adhere to what we Pentecostals believe. My question to you is this: will you negate what you know to be real just because someone else doesn't believe the way you do? Of course not. In fact, you'd probably be smug and say, "Well, they will mature sooner or later or just miss out completely." Is it possible that the opponents of this present move of God—Pentecostal or not—may need to "mature" or "miss out?"

> **Is it possible that the opponents of this present move of God—Pentecostal or not—may need to "mature" or "miss out?"**

I'm not trying to be critical; I'm just pointing out that God may be doing something in our land today that will require us to become totally dependent upon Him because we do not, as of yet, understand everything that is happening. But the fact is that it *is* happening, and it *will continue* to happen.

We are only in the beginning stages of this move, not in the actual fullness itself, and yet it already has the religious society rocking, trying to discredit its authenticity or even declare that it is demonic. The truth is that they just can't handle it! Why? Because it is one of God's suddenlies. It is totally wiping away the prevailing structures and forms, rendering them powerless in its wake! It is accomplishing, in a moment's time, what religion hasn't been able to do in decades. It is healing the soul of man suddenly, when all the counseling, psychiatry and self-help couldn't produce it! It is revealing religious spirits, causing many to turn from religion to God in relationship, receiving life where there was only death before!

> **This is only the beginning. There is an intensity coming that will literally astound everyone!**

"But why all the shaking, laughing, dancing, falling under the power and other manifestations? What's happening?" I submit to you that we are at the dawning of a new day! As that day dawns, God is unleashing His Spirit in the Church once again for His glory and honor. And I am here to say: this is only the beginning. There is an intensity coming that will literally astound everyone, from the youngest to the eldest, the believer and the unbeliever alike. This is only the beginning. More is coming.

Pentecost affected the Church first, but this move of God will go beyond the four walls of the church and into the neighborhoods, cities and nations. First, however, it must move the Body of Christ. The move of God always affects the Church first. Gird yourselves, for the journey is just beginning.

Chapter 4

WHAT'S COMING NEXT?

Then they that gladly received his word were baptized: and the same day there were added unto them about three thousand souls.

Acts 2:41

Howbeit many of them which heard the word believed; and the number of the men was about five thousand.

Acts 4:4

As noted in the previous chapter, the move of God must affect the Church first. It is His plan (and always has been) to minister to His people first. God is a family man. He'll minister to His family first, then enable them to go forth and reach nations for His glory.

Here in Acts, we find that the Church was mightily impacted by God at Pentecost. A bunch of frightened, unsuspecting people, chosen by God for this outpouring, were rained upon by Him, and their lives were never the same again! God made the impact upon them first.

> **A bunch of frightened, unsuspecting people, chosen by God for this outpouring, were rained upon by Him, and their lives were never the same again!**

MY OWN TRANSFORMATION

Through the years, I never succumbed to the temptation to drink or do drugs. Even though I was subjected to seemingly impossible and adverse conditions growing up, I made the choice to enjoy life to its fullest. And, for the most part, with the understanding I had, I have been able to do just that.

I was able to experience the highs of competitive team sports. Going into a football game being the underdogs and coming out on top was an experience that I will never forget.

> **There is nothing quite like the thrill of victory, and very little can satisfy the soul like being considered the least and yet coming out on top!**

I have also enjoyed the thrills of individual competition. Being on the tournament circuit for a couple of years, and being "measured up" before the competition was humorous. I was always the smallest competitor, and yet I had a way of walking away from the competition victorious. There is nothing quite like the thrill of victory, and very little can satisfy the soul like being considered the least and yet coming out on top. It's the David and Goliath thing. I was blessed with the joys of educational opportunities that afforded me privileges that others only dream about.

But none of those things ever moved me like the day God rained Himself down on my life. I was impacted by Him like I had never been impacted by anything before, and it was transformative.

There was a transformation that took place in the early Church after Pentecost. The frightened followers of Christ suddenly took on a mentality that was not their own. Instead of being fearful for their lives, now they were willing to lay their lives down for His sake. Instead of hiding behind closed doors, now they were in the streets proclaiming: *"God hath made that same Jesus, whom ye have crucified, both Lord and Christ"* (Acts 2:36).

> **Their boldness led to them suffering severe persecution, but it also led those who looked on to declare "that they had been with Jesus" (Acts 4:13)!**

What's Coming Next?

The renewed hearts of these humble followers of Christ now propelled them to the forefront of battle with the religious sect of that day, and they did it with a boldness immediately recognized by all who witnessed these events. Their boldness led to them suffering severe persecution, but it also led those who looked on to declare *"that they had been with Jesus"* (Acts 4:13).

I can understand that. The effect of God's impact about in my life, the transformation brought about by His presence with me, has caused me to pursue Him when it seemed the least likely thing to do. Why? Because I know that He is real! When I can't "feel" Him, I am caused to go after Him, just because I know that He is real, know He is there somewhere! This impact on our lives causes us not to be swayed by anything else or turned away from Him. We know that He is real!

The effect of God's impact on my life has kept me from ever having the thought of "throwing in the towel." I do not understand what it is in some people that motivates them to want to turn from God in certain contrary situations, but I do know what could keep them from ever quitting. God can and will so move in your heart and life that you will never have the thought of turning your back on Him.

I bless God that I have never had that thought. I am not saying that I have never fallen, but each time I have, I have not run from Him. Instead, I ran to Him!

Someone may say, "Well, you've never been as low as I have." God forbid that we would measure ourselves among ourselves. We cannot justify our woes by comparing our standings. Let me say to you: Don't concentrate on how low you've been. Instead, get another glimpse on how high God can take you.

> **Don't concentrate on how low you've been. Instead, get another glimpse on how high God can take you!**

The effect of the Spirit's impact on our lives keeps faith and hope alive in us even to the point that when we falter or fail, we are not looking to stay down. We are immediately looking for His hand to lift us up!

The effect of God's impact on our lives keeps us involved in the work that He has called us to and keeps our spirit keen to His bidding.

Friend, I have been hit by a lot of things, but nothing has impacted me more than when God gave me His Spirit. This impacted my life for eternity!

> **I have been hit by a lot of things, but nothing has impacted me more than when God gave me His Spirit!**

THE OUTPOURING

What is it that caused this transformation within the early followers of Christ? I submit to you that it was the outpouring of the Holy Ghost and fire that summoned these people to higher ground. The impartation of God's Spirit upon and within their lives caused them to bridge the chasm between this life and the world to come. Finally, it was the realization of the power of the prayer Jesus taught us to pray, when He said, *"Thy will be done in earth* [in man, as well as on *terra firma*], *as it is in heaven"* (Matthew 6:10). The truth of that reached into the depths of their spirit and ushered them into the power of His might.

> **The Spirit baptism gave them a spiritual backbone, to stand when falling seemed more desirable, to speak boldly when the protocol was to be silent, to act when doing nothing seemed best!**

The baptism of the Holy Spirit did what miracles could not accomplish, what much learning could not do, what years of teaching could not do. The Spirit convinced them of

Christ and their ability to walk in the power of a resurrected Lord and Savior. The Spirit baptism gave them a spiritual backbone, to stand when falling seemed more desirable, to speak boldly when the protocol was to be silent, to act when doing nothing seemed best. The Spirit baptism caused the transformation to take place in their lives that gave birth to the greatest entity on this planet and in the heart of God—His glorious Church!

Although the Spirit-filled Church has had her highs and lows since that day, her good times and her bad times, and although many have abused her gifts and strengths, she has always recovered, not to equal standing, but to far greater than before because she is endued with power from on high. This is the only power that can sustain and propel men into their fullness—the power of the Holy Spirit.

The best teachings I have ever received concerning the baptism of the Holy Spirit came from my spiritual father, Rev. Marvin Gorman of New Orleans, Louisiana. Not only have I received much insight through his teachings, but on the first Monday night of the first week of July, 1967, Brother Gorman ministered the message that totally revolution-ized my life.

After he spoke about the baptism of the Holy Spirit, Brother Gorman gave an altar call, in-viting anyone who wanted to be baptized with this wonderful third Person of the Godhead. As a fifteen-year-old boy, I went forward and was filled with the Holy Ghost and fire. Today, I stand as a living witness of what the Spirit of God can do. He has no equal when it come to transform-ing and impacting a life. He met me to such a degree that my life has never been the same!

> **Today I stand as a living witness of what the Spirit of God can do!**

Pastor Gorman left us for his eternal reward in early 2017, at the age of 83, but before his death, he was still ministering with a heavier-than-ever anointing when he spoke concerning the baptism of the Holy Spirit. Multitudes were filled and received the miraculous works of God in their lives through his ministry.

WHAT'S COMING NEXT?

I believe that there is another impartation of God's Spirit coming to our lives that will make such an impact on the Church that our foundations will literally shake with the reception of His glory. God is about to impact His Church once again with His Spirit!

> **God is about to impact His Church once again with His Spirit!**

I'm talking about an unprecedented outpouring of the Holy Ghost for this generation that will bring such an impact to the Church that she will then go forth and impact the world. As we have noted, the move of God must affect or impact us first. Then, when it has, we will affect and impact the world around us.

In Acts 2 the effects of the Holy Spirit's coming caused three thousand people to come to Christ. In Acts 4, five thousand more came to Him. Then, believers were added daily (see Acts 2:47), then the number multiplied (see Acts 6:1 and 7), and this phenomenal growth continues to this day. All of this speaks to the question: What's Coming?

> **For a long time now the Church has just been picking tomatoes, but harvest is coming!**

A GREAT HARVEST IS COMING

Jesus spoke much about harvest, and the people He spoke to understood what He meant. When He spoke of harvest, He didn't just mean an ear of corn or a stalk of wheat. He was talking about a serious harvest. He spoke of entire fields being reaped.

What's Coming Next?

You don't go into the garden and pick a tomato and call that "harvest." No, that is just a tomato. If, however, you have a field of tomatoes that need picking, and you go in and clean the field out, now that's a harvest. For a long time now the Church has just been picking tomatoes, but harvest is coming!

Please understand, I am not belittling the fact that one soul comes into the Kingdom. There is rejoicing in Heaven when this happens (Luke 15:10), and I would never dismiss it as being small or insignificant. What I am saying is that God is so filling His Church with His Spirit that entire fields will be harvested at one time. Entire families (now that's a field) will be brought in at one time. Entire cities and even entire nations will be reaped for

Harvest time is a happy time. It's a time of celebration, of coming together and enjoying the fruits of our labors!

God's glory, by the power of His Spirit working through the life of the believer.

> ## He is making of us new wineskins so that His harvest will be contained!

Harvest time is a happy time. It's a time of celebration, of coming together and enjoying the fruits of our labors. And this time that God is bringing us into will also be a very happy time, a time of great jubilation. Is it any wonder that joy is upon the Church at this time? We know that something is about to happen, and that causes us to be joyful!

But the Body of Christ must be prepared to receive the harvest. I realize that there is the need, in the physical sense, to be ready to facilitate the harvest, but I speak more of the need of spiritual preparation. I believe that is what the Lord is doing right now, at least in part, with His Church.

It is like a snowball rolling down the hill, picking up speed and more snow as it travels. It is getting bigger and bigger with each and every passing day, and it cannot be stopped, for it is from God!

God isn't bringing His harvest into old, wretched, decrepit barns. Get ready, for His harvest is coming in with joy unspeakable and full of glory. Old wineskins will not be able to accommodate the new wine. So, God is doing something about that in those who will allow Him to. He is making of us new wineskins so that His harvest will be contained. God's Holy Spirit is preparing the Church for the greatest move this planet has ever experienced, the former rain and the latter rain combined.

Preachers, you have been preaching about this for years. You have gotten people excited and given them an expectation of something that is to come. Well, now that it is here, would you dare fight against it? Please don't fight it, for it is what we've been waiting for all along.

God has promised it and, praise His name, the outpouring has begun! It is like a snowball rolling down the hill, picking up speed and more snow as it travels. It is getting bigger and bigger with each and every passing day, and it cannot be stopped, for it is from God!

SOME PRINCIPLES OF HARVEST

Here are some simple principles for harvest:

1. Choose the ground well. The field is the world you live in. Sow into good ground, and you will reap a good harvest.
2. Prepare the ground. Till the ground with prayer, intercession, supplications, witnessing, consistency and persistence.
3. Understand proper seed planting. Timing is everything in harvest. Learn to move with the cloud and lay down seeds in God's timing.

4. Understand proper seed care. Watering, weeding and fertilizing are all vital to a good harvest. Don't neglect them and expect a harvest.

Understand proper seed care. Watering, weeding and fertilizing are all vital to a good harvest. Don't neglect them and expect a harvest!

---

5. Understand proper care of seedlings. Now that you have a life in your care, take every opportunity to instill God into it, enforcing Calvary's victory over the enemy at every turn.

6. Understand harvest time. This is it, what we've been waiting for all along and what God has been preparing us for. He is about to instruct His angels to thrust in the sickle and reap, for He has prepared His earth for this last great harvest.

When will it happen? When you and I are fully impacted by God's Spirit, then we will see it. Get ready!

Chapter 5

THE SIXTH-DAY BLESSING

The same day there came certain of the Pharisees, saying unto him, Get thee out, and depart hence: for Herod will kill thee. And he said unto them, Go ye, and tell that fox, Behold, I cast out devils, and I do cures to day and to morrow, and the third day I shall be perfected. Nevertheless I must walk to day, and to morrow, and the day following: for it cannot be that a prophet perish out of Jerusalem. O Jerusalem, Jerusalem, which killest the prophets, and stonest them that are sent unto thee; how often would I have gathered thy children together, as a hen doth gather her brood under her wings, and ye would not! Behold, your house is left unto you desolate: and verily I say unto you, Ye shall not see me, until the time come when ye shall say, Blessed is he that cometh in the name of the Lord.   Luke 13:31-35

As I was considering the message of this book, the word *expectancy* kept resounding in my spirit. I believe that God is instilling, once again, an expectancy into our hearts concerning Him and His work. Our hunger grows, our vision enlarges, and the former boundaries are no more.

> **I believe that God is instilling, once again, an expectancy into our hearts concerning Him and His work!**

The important issue we are facing today is not how to bring laughter, shaking or other strange phenomena under the power of the Spirit. The issue at hand is a hungry generation fed up with all the religious garb that has left them empty and searching. The issue is God watching over His Word to perform it, as men and women relentlessly seek Him and His presence and power, totally submitting themselves to Him. The issue is God! He has tabernacled among us, and nothing can stop that. It is *His* covenant, *His* desire that hasn't changed because of the fall, to walk with the greatest of His creations—man.

THE IMPORTANCE OF THE COVENANT

I need to say a few words about this matter of covenant. With knowledge comes the opportunity and responsibility for application. Without knowledge, we perish, not in the sense of death, but in the context of having it all but never attaining anything real. This is what the disciples struggled with after the death of Jesus—their unfulfilled destiny, and this is what the church has struggled with for ages—an unfulfilled destiny. Destiny is what God is bringing the church into, His destiny. And that is why there is such a "spiritual rush" to the watering holes.

Our thirst is being quenched, and God is being allowed to manifest His presence. Man is familiar with the omnipresence of the Lord, but it has come time for His manifest presence. That is why there is this rush of unparalleled proportions to these watering holes. Man has been in the desert far too long, and the evidence of the desert in man is his desire to drink. That is exactly what is happening now. Covenant is being renewed between God and His people.

> **Man is familiar with the omnipresence of the Lord, but it has come time for His manifest presence!**

There may be some who will never fully receive the benefits that God alone can provide and which no man can hinder, but multiplied tens of thousands of God's people will receive and live in the abundance of the benefits of their covenant with God. The potential of this people is limitless, and it is God's good pleasure to give us His Kingdom (see Luke 12:32).

> **The Body of Christ has been brainwashed into blaming the devil for everything, even to the extent of being unscriptural!**

The Body of Christ has been brainwashed into blaming the devil for everything, even to the extent of being unscriptural. But the Spirit of God is arising in His people once again, giving us the realization that *"we are of God"* (1 John 4:6 and 5:19). Since we are of God, there is nothing the enemy can do to withstand the force of the Spirit of God in the blood-washed Church.

Neighbor, you can forget your covenant, you can release it and you can fail to appropriate it, but it will be your neglect, not the power of the enemy that keeps you from attaining all that God has promised. This may surprise you, but the devil doesn't have the power to break your covenant with God! Only you do!

> **The devil doesn't have the power to break your covenant with God! Only you do!**

Surrender yourself to the covenant of God and live life to the fullest in Him. His strength will carry you through to the unknown riches available in Him. There is healing for you, strength for you, blessings in abundance for you, deliverance for you and the strength to live abundantly in this life for you through His covenant.

Once again, do not allow the cry of the critic to be greater than the cry of your God. Do not minimize the One who resides within you! We are one of God's divine appointments for this planet.

UNDERSTANDING THE SIXTH DAY

Our text in Luke 13:31-35 contains a prophecy given by Jesus concerning His day, this day that we live in and the last day. I believe there are jewels of knowledge that are even now being revealed concerning our authority as believers, and this is one of them.

According to Romans 8, the creation groans in travail and waits for the manifestation of the sons of God (see verse 22). In essence, the creation is saying to the sons of God, "Come on, Church, get on with the business of God, with the authority He has given you to break the bondages on this earth." Imagine the hosts of Heaven urging us on to do God's bidding.

> **Imagine the hosts of Heaven urging us on to do God's bidding!**

Now, give special attention to what I am about to say, for it will change your life dramatically. If you can hear and apply the Word of the Lord to your life, nothing will be impossible to you.

WHAT WE LEARN FROM BIBLE HISTORY

According to Bible historians, the earth and all that is in it was created in six days and, then, on the seventh day, God rested. This makes the seventh day the day of completion, the perfect day.

Notice that I did *not* say it was the day we are in Heaven or when the Church is raptured out. It is a day of rest.[1] The Word of the Lord is filled with sevens and we are finally coming to understand what they mean.

Another scripture we must look at before we proceed is found in 2 Peter 3:8. It reads:

> *But, beloved, be not ignorant of this one thing, that one day is with the Lord as a thousand years, and a thousand years as one day.*

According to theologians, this scripture can be interpreted a number of different ways. For the sake of time we will look at one of those ways as it applies to our text found in Luke.

---

1. For a better understanding of scriptural rest, order my CD entitled "Resting in the Lord"

According to Bible history, from Adam to Jesus was approximately four thousand years. If we apply the present interpretation of a day being a thousand years and a thousand years being a day, then it would appear to me that the four thousand years between Adam and Jesus would be four days. I wasn't all that hot in math, but I figured that one out pretty fast.

Again, according to Bible historians, from Jesus to today is approximately two thousand years. That equates to two days. Using simple addition, from Adam to now, would be six thousand years or six days. That, by the way, is how I derived the title of this chapter, "The Sixth-Day Blessing."

The "third day" that Jesus refers to in the text (Luke 13:32) is simply *"the day following."* It is actually translated that way in the next verse (verse 33). That would be the seventh day or the next millennium, that day being a day of completion, rest and perfection.

Herod had sent word to Jesus that he would kill Him. Jesus didn't seem too upset about this message, for all He said was to go and tell that

> # He was about to do some things that would totally bring chaos to the realms of darkness!

fox He was about to do some things that would totally bring chaos to the realms of darkness. He said, *"Behold, I cast out devils, and I do cures to day and to morrow, and the third day I shall be perfected"* (verse 32).

Let's examine for just a moment the implications of what Jesus said. He said that He would cast out devils. Simply put, Jesus was going to bring havoc to the kingdom of darkness. Light was going to confront darkness, and darkness would have to flee!

And that is exactly what Jesus did. He conquered the enemy in people's lives and set them free. The possessed, oppressed and depressed, the outcasts and the down-and-outers were all set free from the bondage of the enemy as Jesus went about casting out devils!

Jesus also said that He would *"do cures."* That phrase encompasses every type of miracle of healing known. He went about healing *"all that were oppressed of the devil"* (Acts 10:38). The blind would see, the deaf would hear, the lame would walk, the maimed were made whole, the dead were raised and the captives were set free!

> **The possessed, oppressed and depressed, the outcasts and the down-and-outers were all set free from the bondage of the enemy as Jesus went about casting out devils!**

This is what Jesus did while He lived here on Father's planet. He not only prophesied about it; He lived it in the power of His might. But, that's not all. He didn't only say He would do it in His day (the KJV text calls it *"to day"*); He said He would also do it *"to morrow,"* or the sixth day, our day!

As the Spirit-filled, Spirit-empowered Body of Christ, we are enabled, commissioned by Christ, to *"do cures and cast out devils!"* We are to bring havoc to the kingdom of darkness by being involved in setting men and women free by the power of God. Hell should still be suffering today as a result of the prophetic utterance that Jesus gave to this generation!

We are given authority to do the works that Jesus did—cast out devils and do cures. Now I don't know about you, but that would be enough for me, just knowing what Jesus said He would do and being involved in doing it. But if we stop there, we would have missed the blessing of the sixth day. This blessing is what will usher us into the seventh day, or *"the day following."*

> **We are given authority to do the works that Jesus did—cast out devils and do cures!**

THE DOUBLE PORTION

In Exodus 16:5, there is a mighty truth that begins to give us the understanding of the sixth-day blessing for the people of God:

And it shall come to pass, that on the sixth day they shall prepare that which they bring in; and it shall be twice as much as they gather daily.

As you read this text, it speaks about the provision that God made for His people during the week (the first five days). But notice what transpires on the sixth day. A double portion of all the provisions was to be received on that day. This meant a double portion of all the previous days, because on the seventh day, rest was coming! Imagine, twice as much as the previous days.

We are living in the sixth day (and I might add, nearing the end of the sixth day), and we should be receiving a double portion, twice as much as the previous days, a double portion of the blessings and power of God. We, as the sixth-day people, should be living in a double-portion realm, more than any other day in history. More (double) than Abraham, Isaac, Jacob, Moses, Elijah, Elisha and all the other Bible characters! God has promised a double portion for the sixth day, and we are the sixth-day people!

> **We are living in the sixth day (and I might add, nearing the end of the sixth day), and we should be receiving a double portion, twice as much as the previous days, a double portion of the blessings and power of God!**

HEIRS OF THE PROMISE

In Deuteronomy 21:15-17, we are given some understanding of the heirs and their portion.

The Sixth-Day Blessing

If a man have two wives, one beloved, and another hated, and they have born him children, both the beloved and the hated; and if the firstborn son be hers that was hated: then it shall be, when he maketh his sons to inherit that which he hath, that he may not make the son of the beloved firstborn before the son of the hated, which is indeed the firstborn: but he shall acknowledge the son of the hated for the firstborn, by giving him a double portion of all that he hath: for he is the beginning of his strength; the right of the firstborn is his.

This text describes the portion of *"the firstborn"* as a double portion of all of the father's goods, and this is called *"the right of the firstborn."* Simply put, the right of the firstborn is a double portion of the inheritance.

That's good, but how does that pertain to us? If you will read Hebrews 12:23, you will notice there that we are called *"the church of the firstborn."* And since we are *"the church of the firstborn,"* the right of the firstborn, a double portion, is ours! Hallelujah! Friend, as you begin to realize this truth, your cup will surely run over.

> **Since we are "the church of the firstborn," the right of the firstborn, a double portion, is ours!**

Here is some more understanding found in 2 Kings 2:1-14. Familiarize yourself with this text concerning the transition from Elijah to Elisha. God spoke to both of these two prophets concerning His plan to take Elijah to Heaven. Elijah tried to prevent Elisha from following him, but Elisha refused to leave his side. (I wonder if he had something up his sleeve.)

Finally, Elijah said: *"Ask what I shall do for thee, before I be taken away from thee"* (verse 9).

Elisha answered, *"I pray thee, let a double portion of thy spirit be upon me"* (same verse).

Then Elijah said a very strange thing, *"Thou hast asked a hard thing"* (verse 10). What was so hard about it? Elisha was asking for the portion of the heir. He wanted the right of the firstborn. And that is precisely why it was so hard. He was asking to become Elijah's son. He wanted the double portion, but that was reserved for the heir, the firstborn, and not anyone else, especially not a slave or servant like Elisha. Still, Elijah said that if Elisha would see him taken away, it would be so.

> **He [Elisha] wanted the double portion, but that was reserved for the heir, the firstborn, and not anyone else, especially not a slave or servant like him!**

RECEIVING HIS PORTION

Then, suddenly, a chariot of fire and horses of fire separated the two men, and Elijah was taken to Heaven while Elisha watched him ascend. Then it was Elisha's turn to say something very strange: *"My father, my father, the chariot of Israel and the horsemen thereof"* (verse 12).

What was so strange about that? In that culture, a slave or servant was not allowed to address his master by calling him "father." That term was reserved for the firstborn. But here was Elisha, looking up and calling out, *"My father, my father!"* Something happened when he saw his master being taken up. A transformation took place, changing Elisha from a servant to a son, from a slave to the firstborn! And, therefore, all the rights of the firstborn, the double portion, were now rightfully his.

> **A change took place in me, and I moved from being a slave to being a son of God, from being a servant to sin, to being the firstborn in God's House!**

There was a time in my life when I had no right to address God as Father. I was lost in sin, alienated from the covenants of God and His blessings. Sin had enslaved me, kept me away from these blessings. But then, one day,

I looked up! And when I looked up, a transformation took place. A change took place in me, and I moved from being a slave to being a son of God, from being a servant to sin, to being the firstborn in God's House!

Galatians 4:4-7 says it like this:

> *But when the fulness of the time was come, God sent forth his Son, made of a woman, made under the law, to redeem them that were under the law, that we might receive the adoption of sons. And because ye are sons, God hath sent forth the Spirit of his Son into your hearts, crying, Abba, Father. Wherefore thou art no more a servant, but a son; and if a son, then an heir of God through Christ.*

Romans 8:14-17 speaks of our adoption and then declares that we are *"heirs of God and joint-heirs with Christ"*:

> *For as many as are led by the Spirit of God, they are the sons of God. For ye have not received the spirit of bondage again to fear;*

but ye have received the Spirit of adoption, whereby we cry, Abba, Father. The Spirit itself beareth witness with our spirit, that we are the children of God: and if children, then heirs; heirs of God, and joint-heirs with Christ; if so be that we suffer with him, that we may be also glorified together.

There is so much more that we could say about God's promised blessings, but suffice it to say that this blessing is available for you today as a sixth-day man or woman. There's a double portion awaiting you. Go for it!

> **This blessing is available for you today as a sixth-day man or woman!**

One other Scripture on this is found in John 14:12. These are the words of Jesus:

Verily, verily, I say unto you, He that be-lieveth on me, the works that I do shall he

The Sixth-Day Blessing

[the believer] *do also; and greater works than these shall he* [the believer] *do; because I go unto my Father.*

The word *and* is a conjunction, and a conjunction connects two things, two thoughts. I see here, again, a double portion.

We are all living in the sixth day, but we are not all realizing the sixth-day blessing that has been reserved especially for sixth-day people. Let us open ourselves, as sons and daughters of God, and receive the portion of the heir, for it is in this strength that we will enter the next day, the day following, the seventh day. It is in this strength that God's harvest will be realized. Far too long we have lived below the level of God's expectation for us. Let us arise to the occasion and receive our blessing!

Chapter 6

THE COMING CHURCH

The same day there came certain of the Pharisees, saying unto him, Get thee out, and depart hence: for Herod will kill thee. And he said unto them, Go ye, and tell that fox, Behold, I cast out devils, and I do cures to day and to morrow, and the third day I shall be perfected. Luke 13:31-32

As this generation rapidly closes and the next one enters, there seems to be a change indicated in the Word of the Lord, a change that will facilitate Fathers harvest!

The Coming Church

Without a doubt, Luke 13:31-35 is the most comprehensive of all prophecies given in the Word of God. There is no need for guesswork, for it is plainly expressed and explained in context to the degree that anyone can see its validity.

This scripture points to a time coming not so very far in the distant future. In fact, it speaks of a time within the next few years of this writing. As this generation rapidly closes and the next one enters, there seems to be a change indicated in the Word of the Lord, a change that will facilitate Fathers harvest. For a brief moment, let us examine the coming Church, how we can identify it and what are its most outstanding characteristics.

Examine with me, if you will, the verses found in 2 Corinthians 3:17-18 and 4:6:

Now the Lord is that Spirit: and where the Spirit of the Lord is, there is liberty. But we all, with open face beholding as in a glass the glory of the Lord, are changed into the same image from glory to glory, even as by the Spirit of the Lord.

For God, who commanded the light to shine out of darkness, hath shined in our hearts, to give the light of the knowledge of the glory of God in the face of Jesus Christ.

According to these verses, we are being changed, and they seems to indicate a gradual yet continual change taking place over time. I can only conclude that the reason we are being changed is that we are just not quite pure enough yet.

> **The way we change is by getting into the face of Jesus Christ, until we reflect the same image from glory to glory!**

Another passage that speaks of our change is found in John's first epistle to the churches:

Behold, what manner of love the Father hath bestowed upon us, that we should be called the sons of God: therefore the world knoweth us not, because it knew him not. Beloved, now are we the sons of God, and it doth not yet appear what we shall [shall is the operative word] *be: but we know that, when he shall appear, we shall be like him; for we shall see him as he is.* 1 John 3:1-2

The change that we are going through is bringing us into the image of Christ. The way we change is by getting into the face of Jesus Christ, until we reflect the same image from glory to glory.

Have you ever considered what the Church will be like at the end of the age? Consider this: Every child of promise in the Old Testament came from a barren womb. In Genesis 18, for instance, God had an interlude with Abraham in which he told Abraham that his barren wife Sarah would conceive and give birth to a son. In the process of time, Sarah did conceive and gave birth to a son and named him Isaac.

For many years we have defined Isaac's name to mean "laughter." And, in a sense, it does mean that. But if you will examine his name closely, you will find that it means more than mere laughter. It means "incredible joy." Now there's a difference between laughter and incredible joy, although both are closely associated. This child would live a life of incredible joy as the son of Abraham, a very prosperous man.

> **There's a difference between laughter and incredible joy, although both are closely associated!**

In 1 Samuel 1 and 2, you have another instance where a woman was barren, yet promised a man-child by the Lord. In time, Hannah conceived and gave birth to a son she named Samuel. Samuel's ministry spread over forty years in Israel, and during that time he built schools of the prophets and anointed two kings. In the second instance, that of David, the anointing never left David's life. Samuel also showed Israel what it was like to live in covenant with God.

> **God's people were under the oppression of the Philistines when Samson came on the scene with "strength for deliverance!"**

In Judges 13, an angel of the Lord appeared to a woman who was barren and gave her a word from the Lord that she would conceive and bear a son. In time, the wife of Manoah gave birth to a son she named Samson. Samson's name means "strength for deliverance." But notice who was in bondage when Samson showed up with a ministry of deliverance? Was it God's people or the enemy? It wouldn't take much reading to see immediately that God's people were under the oppression of the Philistines when Samson came on the scene with "strength for deliverance."

The last promised child of the Old Testament who came from a barren womb was birthed by Elizabeth. She gave birth to a son named John, and he became known as John the Baptist.

John the Baptist preached three messages: First, he preached repentance. Let me say to you that when a minister is trying to establish an image, a persona, repentance is not the message he's going to preach. The message of repentance is not a popular one, but John made it work for him.

> **I do know that He will move one more time, and when He does, out of the dead womb of orthodoxy and religion, He will bring birth to the greatest harvest this planet has ever known!**

John's next message was concerning the baptism of the Holy Ghost and fire. In fact, he was the first one to coin that phrase.

John's last message was concerning *"one coming,"* and, with it, he introduced the coming of the Lord Jesus.

The Coming Church

Where is the Church headed to? What is the Church going to be like at the end of the age? What can we expect to be like as a Bible-believing child of God? If you put these four facets that we have just spoken of together, you would begin to get the picture of the coming Church.

I don't know how many more times God will move upon the face of this earth, but I do know that He will move one more time, and when He does, out of the dead womb of orthodoxy and religion, He will bring birth to the greatest harvest this planet has ever known! He will have a Church adorned for her Bridegroom.

How will we be able to identify her? Consider, first of all, that she (the coming Church) will be an Isaac people. We are going to be a people of incredible joy! More than just laughter, we will experience incredible joy. Laughter is contingent upon the external, upon things going right, but the joy of the Lord comes from the Spirit of the Lord and is not based upon any particular circumstance.

In his letter to the Philippians (see Philippians 4:11), Paul said that he had learned to be *"content"* in whatever state he was in. This word *content* does not mean "satisfied and, thus, doing nothing." It means "independent of outside circumstances." Paul's life was not based upon externals, but upon the Holy Spirit residing within him.

> # The coming Church will be a Church with incredible joy!

The coming Church will be a Church with incredible joy. Not only did Isaac have incredible joy; he enjoyed the wealth of his father.

Galatians 3:29 tells us:

> *And if ye be Christ's, then are ye Abraham's seed, and heirs according to the promise.*

We belong to Christ and, therefore, are to enjoy the abundance and prosperity of our Father God.

The coming Church will also be a Church with a prophetic anointing and will live within the realms of the rule and reign of Christ. There is a strong move toward the prophetic realm in these days. We are seeing prophetic preaching, prophetic teaching, prophetic praise and prophetic worship. Spirit utterances and prophetic prayers are also intensifying at an incredible rate and rightly so.

> **The coming Church will also be a Church with a prophetic anointing and will live within the realms of the rule and reign of Christ!**

And, since God has spoken, He will bring it to pass. The prophetic will stand out in the coming Church.

Also, the Church will remain within covenant structure and enjoy the benefits of covenant in an unprecedented way.

The coming Church will operate with the Samson ministry of deliverance. God is going to set His world free by setting His people free. Remember, when Samson came on the scene, it was God's people who were in bondage. God sent the ministry of deliverance to His people first.

Today, God's people are so loaded down with baggage that is difficult for them to live according to the liberty of the Word. He will set them free. The chains that seem to bind you will be broken because of Calvary's work being appropriated in your life.

> **The coming Church will operate with the Samson ministry of deliverance!**

Finally, the coming Church will have the spirit of John the Baptist at work in it. Repentance will once again become a bulwark in the House of the Lord. Repentance is a message that must be preached and lived in order that the world can see the freedom of the Lord. Along with repentance, the infilling of and work of the Holy Spirit in the lives of the believer will become evident.

The Holy Ghost will be accompanied by fire, as it was in the early church. The fire of God is coming once again upon His people.

> **Repentance is a message that must be preached and lived in order that the world can see the freedom of the Lord!**

We, like John, will be a people who point others to the coming of the Lord. I do not know what your eschatology is concerning the coming of the Lord. With so many differing views existing today, maybe you're not even sure yourself. But there's one thing we can all agree on, and it is that He is coming again! The coming Church will point people to *"one coming."*

It is an exciting age that we are living in, as the Church becomes what she has been designed to be from its inception in the heavenlies. As John concluded:

> It doth not yet appear what we shall be: but we know that, when he shall appear, we shall be like him; for we shall see him as he is.
>
> 1 John 3:2

AMEN!

AUTHOR CONTACT PAGE

On the Web:
http://jerryfitchministries.com/

E-mail:
decajun2@aol.com

Phone:
(337) 831-0536

Mail:
Jerry and Monique Fitch
4204 Eldridge Street
New Iberia, LA 70563

BOOKS BY JERRY FITCH

Seasons of Suddenlies

...and other revelations of God's times and seasons

by Dr. Jerry Fitch

Introduction by Dr. Jerry Edmon

Moving
through
a Season
of Grief

You have turned my mourning into joyful dancing.
You have taken away my clothes of mourning and clothed me with joy.
Psalm 30:11

Jerry Fitch

THE

FINAL
CALL

ARE WE PRESENTLY RECEIVING THE FINAL CALL OF THE SPIRIT?

JERRY FITCH

COMMUNION

TRUTH
VS.
TRADITION

JERRY FITCH

www.ingramcontent.com/pod-product-compliance
Lightning Source LLC
Chambersburg PA
CBHW051830040426
42447CB00006B/451